Farms

Published 2010 by A&C Black Publishers Limited
36 Soho Square, London W1D 3QY
www.acblack.com

ISBN 978-1-4081-2666-0

Text © Keri Finlayson 2010
Design © Lynda Murray
Photographs © Fotolia
Cover photos © Shutterstock 2010
A CIP record for this publication is available from the British Library.

Printed in Great Britain by Latimer Trend & Company Limited

This book is produced using paper that is made from wood grown
in managed, sustainable forests. It is natural, renewable and
recyclable. The logging and manufacturing processes conform to
the environmental regulations of the country of origin.

To see our full range of titles visit
www.acblack.com

Contents

The 'Let's talk about' series

Communication is vital. The ability to communicate and the ability to comprehend are the most important skills we can foster in young children. Without the ability to speak clearly, listen carefully, and comprehend fully a child's ability to develop literacy and numeracy, and to understand the world around them is compromised.

The 'Let's talk about' series reflects the aims of the Every Child a Talker initiative and promotes verbal communication skills within an environment where children can enjoy experimenting with language. It aims to give those who work with children in the early years, tools for phonological instruction and to offer entertaining, exciting and stimulating activities that foster early language learning. Each book focuses on a popular Early Years theme. The theme is used throughout the book, allowing the practitioner to create a day's activity or a week or term long project.

Speaking and listening are skills that are essential for the development of reading and writing. The ability to articulate clearly is extremely important when acquiring, developing and understanding spoken and written language. The clear and correct pronunciation of words enhances a child's phonological awareness (the ability to distinguish the sounds that make up words) and this in turn promotes the understanding of spelling patterns that will be an essential part of literacy success later on.

Communication Matters: Strands of Communication and Language (DfES 2005) states that:
"There is much variation in the ages in which children who are developing normally learn about features of communication and language. As they are learning, they will also tend to concentrate on particular things at particular ages. So, in infancy they concentrate on the sound patterns of the language; as toddlers they focus on learning words and putting them together; and as young children they learn to extend their proficiency as communicators in a wide range of situations. However, although they might concentrate on different things at different times each is important throughout."

The 'Let's Talk about' Series has been designed with this development across and within strands in mind, and will encourage children to:

- Know and use sounds and signs.

- Know and use words.

- Structure language.

- Make language work.

Using this book

In this book you will discover games that get tongues twisting and lips smacking! There are activities that teach creative communication and foster creative expression, and short plays in age appropriate language that encourage children to become confident and clear communicators. Most of the activities involve lots of chatter and some involve lots of noise!

The activities are suitable for small groups of children, as well as whole class groups. Children have varying attention spans, development rates and areas of interest. You can lengthen, shorten or adapt the activities according to your professional judgement.

The topic of farms provides the early years practitioner with a wealth of ideas. It covers a wide range of early learning goals in areas from Literacy and Numeracy to Knowledge and Understanding of the World.

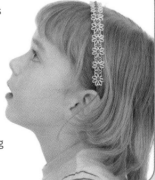

Communication friendly settings

Creating the right environment

Early years practitioners know how important it is to create a setting that encourages children to communicate with each other and with the adults who look after them. This is not always easy in the hustle and bustle of an early years setting. There are many demands on a practitioner's attention and children often raise their voices to be heard or rely on physical cues to communicate needs. By creating a word-sound-rich environment where word sounds are readily heard, children learn that spoken words can do many things. They learn that spoken words convey instructions, describe the physical world around them, and that spoken language enables them to describe their own thoughts feelings, needs and wants.

Developing language and listening skills are fostered by creative exploration and play. Language games, storytelling, dialogic reading, poetry and performance are all excellent ways of doing this and the environment in which these activities take place is very important.

In this section you will find suggestions on how to create an environment that will:

✓ Foster, extend and explore spoken language in your setting.

✓ Encourage confident and articulate conversations between children.

✓ Foster listening and aural discrimination skills.

✓ Allow children to feel relaxed and confident with their speech.

The ideas in this section, as is in the rest of the book, are based around the theme of farms but they can be adapted to suit your needs and preferences.

Some general tips and suggestions

Talking together

Speaking and listening well is not just something we encourage children to do – it is something we must also do well ourselves. This isn't always easy in a busy early years setting, but early years practitioners know that they are role models for active listening and active learning. The way in which we speak to children who are beginning to develop language is vital.

Remember to:

★ **Be seen**

Children need to be able to see our faces and to hear our voices clearly. When speaking to a young child it's important to bend or kneel down if possible. Keep a small cushion near by to kneel on when talking; it could save your knees and your back!

★ **Be expressive**

If your face is lively and animated then you will communicate enthusiasm to the children and they will watch your face closely. The children you are talking to are absorbing the way you form words and are learning new vocabulary all the time.

★ **Be focused**

Make sure that speaking is the only task you are performing. It is easy to slip into the habit of speaking while engaged in another task, such as marking, recording, reading, or even using a computer. It is vitally important that communication is always the priority.

Making conversation – the practitioner as model

Conversation is at the heart of speaking and listening. We all enjoy a friendly, funny, or informative conversation, and we all appreciate it when a conversation is well mannered. As a practitioner you are able to show the children in your care how to conduct a conversation well by:

- Showing genuine interest in what a child tells you.
- Asking a question to follow up what a child has said.
- Adding a fact about your own views or interests.
- If a child asks you a follow up question, expressing pleasure in the fact that they have shown an interest in you.
- If you feel a child wants to talk at length, one to one, try to make time to do this.

Being a good listener

Encourage your children to identify and articulate what makes a good listener and a good speaker themselves. By reflecting on what makes for good speaking and listening and then sharing their thoughts with a group, a child develops a sense of ownership over the task. By identifying problems or difficulties themselves, a child can focus on improving their own skills and assisting

others with theirs. Good speaking goes hand in hand with good listening. By listening carefully children learn to:

- Follow instructions.
- Comprehend what is happening around them.
- Appreciate what is expected of them.
- Understand the thoughts and perspectives of others.
- Learn information.
- Learn language structure and vocabulary.
- Make friends.

Dealing with interruptions

cock-a-doodle-doo!

There are many ways of teaching children not to interrupt or call out and most practitioners develop their own techniques. Raising a hand and then speaking when given permission to do so is the most popular where groups of children are involved. This is a tried and tested method and works well. However, it is obviously not appropriate in all contexts. Imagine if you were asked to raise your hand before speaking during a dinner with friends or while having a conversation with a shopkeeper!

Try using 'Cock-a-doodle the interrupting cockerel' to demonstrate the effect interrupting has on others so that children understand the reason why we raise our hands when talking

in a group, or why we allow others to finish speaking before we start. All you need is a cockerel puppet/toy that interrupts you when you are talking with a loud cock-a-doodle-doo! Show how irritated you are with his interruptions and ask him to stop and the children will soon begin to understand what you are talking about!

Making special places

Creating screened off or enclosed spaces for talk, allows children to develop scenarios without distraction and to practise important conversation skills. This can be tricky if your setting is a pack-away one in a large open space such as a hall. If your setting doesn't naturally lend itself to private spaces you could:

- Screen off a corner by draping a sheet over two chairs and pegging them in place.

- If you are able, fix two hooks on to the two walls that form a corner, stretch a wire or string (well above head height) from the hooks and drape a sheet over it (fixed with clothes pegs).

- Purchase or borrow pop up play tents or beach tents that can be placed anywhere in the setting.

- Collect large cardboard boxes and stack them to form special places.

- Tables can be sat under – cover with a large sheet to create more privacy. (Don't put anything on top of the table that could fall on a child if the sheet is pulled down.)

- Large sheets of cardboard can be leant against a wall to create a 'lean to'. Place a box of books at the base to stop it slipping down.

- Use boxes of books to mark off a corner space.

- Young children are adept at creating their own private spaces or dens. Offer them sheets, boxes and plastic clothes pegs and see what they come up with themselves!

- See also the *A Place to Talk* series by Featherstone for lots more ideas on creating communication friendly spaces.

Storytelling and story making areas

Children learn so much from listening to stories. You can enhance their experience by creating special spaces for storytelling and story making. Make a space that can be transformed in minutes into a calm place for focused listening and then into a stimulating environment for retelling and narrative based play.

Story time traditionally is an activity that takes place at the end of a session. Try telling a story at the beginning of a session to directly inspire play. Provide props and costumes that relate to the story then encourage some children to stay in the story space while you withdraw.

De-clutter, re-clutter

De-clutter your story space so it doesn't distract from the narrative. When you are telling a story all eyes should ideally be on you. Make focusing easy for little listeners by minimizing visual distractions.

Re-clutter the space with relevant materials to prompt retelling or narrative based play. Place chosen material in the area after you have finished telling the story. Children can then use the materials as props and prompts to retell the story or engage in role-play.

Keep it quiet

Early years settings are noisy places, with plenty of laughter, shouts, bangs and crashes. However, during story time, make sure that the only sounds heard are the voices of those telling the story. Minimize noise levels by either telling a story to the whole group or by engaging non-story listening children in quieter activities.

Whispers only

The sounds of speech can sometimes be lost if the noise level is too high. Try creating a corner that is 'whispers only' for a reason, such as all the baby animals on the farm are going to sleep.

In this activity children can spend time in a quiet area where communication is encouraged through a participatory activity but voices are kept low so that they are focused on listening carefully to each other. By encouraging quiet, one to one conversation you are allowing the children to practise turn-taking techniques and to develop essential listening skills.

What you need

- ✓ Blankets, cushions and pillows
- ✓ Toy farm animals
- ✓ Hair brushes
- ✓ Small plastic bowls
- ✓ Toy beds and cots if available

Talk about...

- ★ The children's own bedtime routines.
- ★ What makes us sleepy?
- ★ Dreams. What do we dream about? What might horses or cows dream about?

What you do

- Decide on an area that is going to be the day's 'whispers only' area and arrange the blankets and cushions within it. A corner is often best.
- Collect toy farm animals (soft toys or toys from small world play). You could ask children to bring in toy farm animals of their own. (Remember to keep a note of who owns each toy.)
- Explain to the children that there is a place in your setting where the baby animals like to go to sleep.
- Discuss the fact that animals like to be fed and groomed (brushed) before they go to sleep.
- Place the blankets, brushes and bowls in the 'sleeping area'.
- Allow pairs or small groups of children to put the animals to sleep, reminding them that the animals need people to whisper when they are in the corner because they are very tired.
- Children can feed and groom the sleepy animals as they put them to bed.
- Encourage the children to chat quietly to each other while they carry out the activity.

Links

CLL LfC. 40+m
- Interact with others, negotiating plans and activities and taking turns in conversation.

CD DI&IP. 40+m
- Play along side other children who are engaged in the same theme.

Hunting for eggs

This activity encourages a pair of children to sit quietly together and have a conversation. It is particularly useful for encouraging more reticent children to feel comfortable. Simple activities, such as taking it in turns to use a particular coloured pen, can really help to develop important language skills. By stating that they would like to use a particular coloured pen next, waiting until their partner has finished completing their task and negotiating the use of materials children learn to express their needs clearly and patiently.

What you need

- ✓ A pop up play tent/beach tent/private space
- ✓ Cushions
- ✓ Empty egg cartons
- ✓ Hard boiled eggs (12)
- ✓ A large box
- ✓ Shredded newspaper
- ✓ Jumbo felt tips – one of each colour

What you do

- Fill a large box with shredded newspaper.
- Add the hard boiled eggs.
- Place the box in the tent along with the cushions and some jumbo felt tips.
- Two children can then sit in the 'barn' and hunt in the box for the eggs.
- When found, children can decorate the eggs using the felt tips and place them in the egg boxes.
- Before the children start the activity explain that though there are plenty of felt pens, there is only one of each colour so they will have to share and take turns.

Talk about...

- ★ Where eggs come from.
- ★ Explain that chickens lay eggs in straw and that the farmer collects the eggs from the straw.
- ★ Ways to eat eggs.
- ★ Turn taking and the importance of not snatching.

Links

CLL LfC. 40+m

- Interact with others, negotiating plans and activities and taking turns in conversation.

CLL LfC. 40+m

- Have confidence to speak to others about their own wants and interests.

* Remember to explain that the eggs we eat do not contain chicks.

Grooming horses

In the past, certain early years activities have been perceived as gender specific i.e. suitable for boys only or for girls only. Assumptions were perhaps made about girls enjoying quiet, caring or decorative activities while boys enjoyed more active play. This, some have argued led to girls becoming better at particular types of communication. We can avoid this by encouraging boys and girls equal access to a range of activities that demand different communication styles and techniques.

Make your own stables complete with grooming materials to encourage quiet focused conversation. Pairs of children share a horse to groom – one decorating the tail, the other the mane. If toy horses are not available for the activity, try making your own horses to groom (see page 11 for instructions).

(see page 11 for instructions)

What you need

- ✓ A toy horse with brushable mane and tail or make your own (see P11).
- ✓ A pop up play/beach tent/ private area to act as the stable
- ✓ Cushions
- ✓ Brushes and combs
- ✓ Rubber bands or small 'scrunchies'
- ✓ Beads with large holes

What you do

- Place the toy horse, cushions brushes and combs in the stable.
- Show the children how to groom a horse's mane and tail.
- Explain that sometimes people like to decorate manes and tails with ribbons or beads.
- Demonstrate that beads can be threaded onto the tail and secured beneath with elastic bands.
- Some older children may be able to plait. Encourage them to show others how to plait too. Remember, plaiting, threading beads and other fine motor skill activities are not just for girls!

Links

PSE D&A. 40+m
- Persist for extended periods of time at an activity of their choosing.

PSE MR. 30-50m
- Demonstrate flexibility and adapt their behaviour to different events and changes in routine.

Communication friendly settings

Make your own horse to groom

What you need

- ✓ Very thick card (e.g. corrugated card)
- ✓ Wool
- ✓ Strong glue

What you do

- Draw the outline of a horse on to the card and cut it out. You can make the horse as small or large as you like.
- Cut the wool into strands.
- Glue strands to the head and neck of the horse to make the mane.
- Add strands to make the tail.

Talk about...

- ★ The fact that horses have long manes and tails and these can be brushed and combed to make them smooth and shiny and to keep them clean.
- ★ The ways in which we care for our own hair.
- ★ Different ways of styling or decorating hair.
- ★ Names for horses.

Farm appliqué backdrops

Appliqué is a simple and effective way of creating a themed backdrop for a story area. Cut and then sew fabric shapes on to a cotton sheet to create a farmyard scene. Peg it from a washing line, drape over a table or place on the floor and use it as a play mat. Hang with the plain side visible when telling the story, then reverse to show images to stimulate story based play. Appliquéd sheets can also be pegged outside on a fence to take the scene outside.

What you do

- Decide with the children the scene you would like to create. You may want animals, tractors, farm buildings and even a pond with ducks.
- Search for inspiration in books, magazines, and online or just use your imagination.
- Draw and cut templates of the items in your scene. Make them large - remember they are going to be placed on a large sheet.
- Pin the templates to your chosen fabric and cut around (you).
- When you have all the fabric shapes for your scene ask the children to position the shapes on the sheet and then pin and stitch in place (you).
- You can use a simple running stitch to sew the farm shapes in place. Bright thick thread in a contrasting colour looks particularly effective.

What you need

- ✓ A plain bed sheet
- ✓ Felt
- ✓ Assorted fabric scraps
- ✓ Pins
- ✓ Sharp, large-eyed needle
- ✓ Thick thread or darning wool
- ✓ Card or paper for templates

Another idea

You could also make farm themed cushion covers for your story area.

Look for cushions with plain covers in local charity shops and appliqué with felt farm animals or other farmyard items.

Bales of hay!

What you need

✓ Empty cardboard boxes
✓ Yellow and brown paint
✓ Thick paintbrushes
✓ Protective sheeting or newspaper

Empty cardboard boxes are very useful for creating enclosed spaces for story telling and play. Collect some large cardboard boxes and turn them into hay bales and build yourself a cosy space in amongst them.

What you do

- Fold the boxes shut if possible rather than tape them, they are then open to other play possibilities when their time as 'hay bales' is at en end.

- Show the children how to paint the boxes with brown and yellow stripes and splodges to turn them into bales of hay.

- When dry, use them to turn any area into a barn or farmyard.

Talk about...

★ How hay is made

Hay is made from dried grass. Grass is cut in late summer when it's tall and green. It's then left to dry. When it's dry a special machine makes it into hay bales.

★ What hay is used for

Hay is used as food and bedding for animals. Farm animals can eat hay during the winter when there is little green grass growing in the fields.

★ Where hay is stored

Hay is stored in hay barns. It's important that hay is kept dry. If it gets wet it will go soggy and animals can't eat it.

Links

CD EMM. 30-50m

- Begin to construct, stacking blocks vertically and horizontally, making enclosures and creating spaces.

Shout it out!

Children love poetry. They find language patterns fun and will spontaneously create and play with rhyme, rhythm, assonance and alliteration so poetry is an ideal vehicle for developing language and literacy skills and for learning about our natural, physical, social, personal and numerical world. Children who have an understanding of rhyme and rhythm have an enriched understanding of language and feel confident and creative with literacy.

In this section you will find a variety of farm themed rhymes, poems and activities. Each rhyme is accompanied by the following:

✓ Warm up activities to get mouths and bodies ready to rhyme!

✓ Tips on how to learn the rhyme together.

✓ Things to talk about relating to the rhyme that can be used in adult led discussion.

✓ Lists of words that may be new to all or some. These words can be explored for sound and meaning.

★ Enunciate clearly

When you recite a rhyme with children they look to your face for visual pronunciation cues. Over emphasize any tricky sounds. Be aware of the shapes your mouth is making.

★ Look around

Your face is very important – make sure everyone can see it. If the children are seated on the floor around you, make eye sweeps, turning your face from one side of the group to the other so every child gets a chance to see your face as you say the poem. Remember those closest to your feet may have the most restricted view.

Some general tips and suggestions

Why learn 'by heart'?

Rhymes are easy to memorize so information and vocabulary embedded in rhymes are remembered too. Learning to recite a short poem 'by heart' gives a child confidence. Reciting a short poem to adult friends, carers or family members gives a child a chance to perform, receive praise and feel comfortable speaking in front of others.

Some children love reciting rhymes in front of others while other children enjoy chanting rhymes as part of a group. Use your professional judgement and your knowledge of the children in your care to decide who might enjoy solo or group performances or who would perhaps feel more confident later in the year.

Remember to...

★ Move your body

Learning to recite rhymes is fun. Communicate your enthusiasm for rhyme and rhythm by moving your own body in time to the rhythm; clap your hands, stamp your feet, sway in time. Body movement is an important part of active learning.

Using farm rhymes

Many traditional nursery rhymes are based on the theme of farms. Children in your setting may know rhymes and songs with a farm theme that they have learnt at home.

Make a recording of farm-themed nursery rhymes

You could ask parents and carers if they can contribute farm rhymes of their own. Also ask your children if they know any farm rhymes in a language other than English. Make a recording of all the different versions and use it in your setting for listening activities.

Invite nursery rhyme 'listeners' to your setting

Invite parents and carers to visit your setting as 'listeners'. Explain to the visiting adults that their job is to listen to individual or groups of children recite rhymes and provide positive and appreciative feedback. If your setting is attached to or contained within a primary school, you could arrange for older children to help out as listeners.

If appropriate, you could put on a formal performance, but with younger children it is often better for the adult to move freely and informally around the setting to listen to individual or small groups of children. Make badges for your invited listeners so that the children can identify them as people who are ready to listen to their rhymes. You could make badges in the shape of an ear.

Popular farm nursery rhymes		
Ba Ba Black Sheep	Little boy blue	There was an old lady who swallowed a fly
Little Bo Peep	Sing a song of sixpence	This little piggy went to market
Mary had a little lamb	Old MacDonald had a farm	

Clip clop horsey

Clip clop horsey

Clip, clop horsey walking down the lane.
(clip, clop, clip, clop)

Clip, clop horsey walking back again.
(clip, clop, clip, clop)

Clip, clop horsey walking up the hill.
(clip, clop, clip, clop)

Clip, clop horsey try to stand still!
(clip, clop, clip, clop)

This activity enables children to:

✓ Focus on the 'cl' sound.

✓ Practise producing a regular rhythm.

✓ Learn about the horse as an animal.

✓ Explore horse related vocabulary.

What you do

Warm up

- Practise clapping in time. This can be tricky for very young children. Start with clapping very slowly to the count of four.
- Practise the 'cl' sound. Say the word 'clap' when clapping with your hands.

Activity

- Recite the rhyme.
- Ask the children to recite the rhyme with you, clapping 'clip, clop, clip, clop' at the end of each line.
- Move about as you recite the rhyme. Walk around as horses for the first three lines, then stand still for the last line.

Links

CLL LfC. 30-50m

- Join in with repeated refrains and anticipate key events and phrases in rhymes and stories.

CLL LfC. 40+m

- Listen with enjoyment and respond to stories, songs, music rhymes and poems and make up their own stories, songs rhymes and poems. (ELG)
- Extend their vocabulary, exploring the meanings and sounds of words.

CD CM&D. 30-50m

- Sing a few familiar songs.
- Explore and learn how sounds can be changed.

Talk about...

★ What colours can horses be?

★ How many legs do they have?

★ Discuss the names for different parts of a horse's body. How could we describe them?

★ Discuss what equipment we need to ride them.

★ What do horses eat?

★ Where do they live?

★ What is a young horse called?

Vocabulary

foal   hoof   mane   saddle   bridle   reins

Shout it out!

This is the way

This activity is best carried out where there is plenty of space to move around.

This is the way the ladies ride,
Gallopy, gallopy, gallopy, gallopy.
This is the way the gentlemen ride,
Trit, trot, trit, trot.
This is the way the children ride,
Wibbly, wobbly
Wibbly, wobbly
Wibbly, wobbly, woo!

Talk about...

★ The words that describe human movement e.g. hop, walk, run, jump.

★ The different speeds at which a horse can run.

★ Introduce the words 'gallop' and 'trot.'

wibbly wobbly woo!

This activity enables children to:

✓ Use movement with rhyme.

✓ Explore descriptions of movement.

✓ Focus on producing the 'w' sound.

What you do

Warm up

- Practise making the 'w' sound. The 'w' sound is fun to make. Try saying 'why, why, why'.

- Practise moving like a horse:

- Gallop by running quickly.

- Trot on your toes.

- Sway from to side to side as you wobble around.

Activity

- Read the rhyme.

- Read the rhyme a second time telling the children to gallop, trot and wobble as they say it.

- Find a space and practise your galloping, trotting and wobbling.

Links

CLL LfC. 30-50m

- Join in with repeated refrains and anticipate key events and phrases in rhymes and stories.

CLL LfC. 40+m

- Listen with enjoyment and respond to stories, songs, music rhymes and poems and make up their own stories, songs rhymes and poems. (ELG)

- Extend their vocabulary, exploring the meanings and sounds of words.

CD CM&D. 30-50m

- Sing a few familiar songs.

- Explore and learn how sounds can be changed.

Vocabulary

gallop   trot   wobble

It's time to feed the cows

It's time to feed the cow.   *Moo!*
It's time to feed the cow.   *Moo!*
Munch, munch, munch, munch!
It's time to feed the cow.   *Moo!*

It's time to milk the cow.   *Moo!*
It's time to milk the cow.   *Moo!*
Splash, splash, splash, splash!
It's time to milk the cow.   *Moo!*

It's time to drink the milk.   *Moo!*
It's time to drink the milk.   *Moo!*
Slurp, slurp, slurp, slurp!
It's time to drink the milk.   *Moo!*

Links

CLL LfC. 30-50m

- Join in with repeated refrains and anticipate key events and phrases in rhymes and stories.

CLL LfC. 40+m

- Listen with enjoyment and respond to stories, songs, music rhymes and poems and make up their own stories, songs rhymes and poems. (ELG)
- Extend their vocabulary, exploring the meanings and sounds of words.

CD CM&D. 30-50m

- Sing a few familiar songs.
- Explore and learn how sounds can be changed.

This activity enables children to:

- ✓ Learn about cows.
- ✓ Speak with rhythm.
- ✓ Practise the initial 'm' sound.

What you do

Warm up

- Practise your moo-ing!
- Put your lips together and see how loudly you can moo.

Activity

- Read the rhyme asking the children to join in with the moos.
- Read a second time with the children joining in all the way.
- Now practise to make perfect!

Talk about...

- ★ What cows look like.
- ★ What colours can they be?
- ★ Where do they live?
- ★ What do they eat?
- ★ Why do we keep cows?

moo!

Vocabulary

munch   splash   slurp

Shout it out!

Maisy Moo

I had a cow.
Her name was Maisy.
She could be a little crazy.
So I called her...
Crazy Maisy.

I had a cow
Her name was Maisy.
She liked to munch upon a daisy.
So I called her...
Daisy Maisy.

I had a cow.
Her name was Maisy.
Sometimes she was very lazy.
So I called her...
Lazy Maisy.

Crazy Maisy.
Daisy Maisy.
Lazy Maisy.

Moo!

This activity enables children to:

✓ Tell a story through a poem.

✓ Practise the long 'a' sound.

✓ Learn about rhyme.

What you do

Warm up

- Practise making the long 'a' sound. Make it really long.
- Say 'a a play away, a a stay away'.

Activity

- Read the rhyme, stressing the long 'a' sound.
- Talk about the words that rhyme with Maisy.
- Perform the rhyme together, stretching out the long 'a' sounds.

Talk about...

★ What cows look like.

★ What names you would choose for a cow.

★ What does a daisy look like?

Vocabulary

munch   lazy   daisy

Links

CLL LfC. 30-50m

· Join in with repeated refrains and anticipate key events and phrases in rhymes and stories.

CLL LfC. 40+m

· Listen with enjoyment and respond to stories, songs, music rhymes and poems and make up their own stories, songs rhymes and poems. (ELG)

· Extend their vocabulary, exploring the meanings and sounds of words.

CD CM&D. 30-50m

· Sing a few familiar songs.

· Explore and learn how sounds can be changed.

Tractor

I'm a big green tractor.
I've got big black wheels.
I pull heavy bales of hay,
All around the fields.
Brmmmmm!

I'm a big green tractor.
I've got big black wheels.
I carry lots of yummy food,
For animals to eat.
Brmmmmm!

I'm a big green tractor.
I've got big black wheels.
I have a very noisy horn,
Jump up and give a beep.
Beeeeep!

This activity enables children to:

✓ Practise the initial 'b' sound.

✓ Practise the sound 'br'.

✓ Learn about tractors.

✓ Role-play inanimate objects.

What you do

Warm up

• Practise the 'b' and 'br' sound.

Say: brrrrr, brrrrr, brrrrr

Say: bob, bob, bob

Activity

• Read the poem through asking the children to join in with the 'brmm' and 'beep' sounds.

• As you read emphasize the 'b' sound at the beginning of the words 'big' and 'black'.

• Practise reciting the poem together.

Talk about...

★ Tractors. Can you describe a tractor?

★ What jobs do they do?

Links

CLL LfC. 30-50m

· Join in with repeated refrains and anticipate key events and phrases in rhymes and stories.

CLL LfC. 40+m

· Listen with enjoyment and respond to stories, songs, music rhymes and poems and make up their own stories, songs rhymes and poems. (ELG)

· Extend their vocabulary, exploring the meanings and sounds of words.

CD CM&D. 30-50m

· Sing a few familiar songs.

· Explore and learn how sounds can be changed.

Vocabulary

heavy   noisy   tractor

Shout it out!

Farm cats

We are a gang of farm cats.
A gang of furry farm cats.
We slink and slide
And creep and crawl,
Under gates and over walls.
Miaowwwww.

We are a gang of farm cats.
A gang of furry farm cats.
We leap and pounce
And stretch our paws,
Over ledges and under doors.
Miaowwwww

We are a gang of farm cats.
A gang of furry farm cats.
We jump and bounce
And spring and glide,
The mice had better run and hide!
Miaowwwwww

miaowwwww!

Links

CLL LfC. 30-50m
- Join in with repeated refrains and anticipate key events and phrases in rhymes and stories.

CLL LfC. 40+m
- Listen with enjoyment and respond to stories, songs, music rhymes and poems and make up their own stories, songs rhymes and poems. (ELG)
- Extend their vocabulary, exploring the meanings and sounds of words.

CD CM&D. 30-50m
- Sing a few familiar songs.
- Explore and learn how sounds can be changed.

This activity enables children to:

✓ Learn about words that describe movement.

✓ Explore different kinds of movement.

✓ Practise the 'm' sound.

What you do

Warm up

- Discuss cats: Who owns a cat? What do they look like? How do they move?
- Practise making the 'm' sound. Press your lips together and say mmmmm.

Activity

- Read the poem aloud.
- Say the poem together making long 'miaow' sounds after each verse.
- Pretend to be farm cats as you recite the poem.

Talk about...
★ Who owns a cat?
★ What do they look like?
★ How do they move?
★ What do they eat?

Vocabulary

slide   creep   crawl   leap   pounce

Wellington boots

I'm on the farm in my Wellington boots.

Stomp, stomp!

Stomp, stomp, stomp!

I'm in the mud in my Wellington boots.

Squelch, squelch!

Squelch, squelch, squelch!

I'm in a puddle in my Wellington boots.

Splash, splash!

Splash, splash, splash!

This activity enables children to:

- ✓ Develop a sense of rhythm.
- ✓ Practise initial blends with 's'.
- ✓ Discuss clothing and its use.

What you do

Warm up

- Practise making the 's' sound. Can you hiss like a snake?
- Practise stomping, squelching and splashing.

Activity

- Read through the poem emphasizing the 's' sound in stomp, squelch and splash.
- Read through again with the children joining in.
- Now recite the poem as you march around stomping, squelching and splashing.

Talk about...

- ★ Wellington boots. Who has a pair at home?
- ★ What do they look like?
- ★ Why do we wear them?
- ★ What is mud?
- ★ When do puddles form?

Links

CLL LfC. 30-50m

- Join in with repeated refrains and anticipate key events and phrases in rhymes and stories.

CLL LfC. 40+m

- Listen with enjoyment and respond to stories, songs, music rhymes and poems and make up their own stories, songs rhymes and poems. (ELG)
- Extend their vocabulary, exploring the meanings and sounds of words.

CD CM&D. 30-50m

- Sing a few familiar songs.
- Explore and learn how sounds can be changed.

Vocabulary

stomp squelch splash mud puddle

Shout it out!

Little hen

Little hen, little hen
Lay an egg for me.
Little hen, little hen
I want one for my tea.
Make it brown,
Or make it white.
I just want an egg tonight.

This activity enables children to:

✓ Learn about chickens and eggs.

✓ Experience rhyme.

✓ Practise the initial 'l' sound.

What you do

Warm up

- Practise making the initial 'l' sound.
- Try saying: la la la.
- Try saying: I like licking lollies.

Activity

- Read through the poem emphasizing the initial 'l' sound.
- Read through again with the children.
- Practise until you know it off by heart.

Talk about...

★ The fact that chickens lay eggs.

★ The ways in which eggs can be cooked.

★ Who likes boiled eggs? Fried eggs? Scrambled eggs?

Links

CLL LfC. 30-50m

- Join in with repeated refrains and anticipate key events and phrases in rhymes and stories.

CLL LfC. 40+m

- Listen with enjoyment and respond to stories, songs, music rhymes and poems and make up their own stories, songs rhymes and poems. (ELG)
- Extend their vocabulary, exploring the meanings and sounds of words.

CD CM&D. 30-50m

- Sing a few familiar songs.
- Explore and learn how sounds can be changed.

Vocabulary

brown white little

Pigs can...

Pigs can oink!
Pigs can zoink!
Pigs can doink!
When they want some food.

Pigs can squeak!
Pigs can eek!
Pigs can squeal!
When they want some food.

Oink, oink, oink!
Squeak, squeak, squeal.
I hear pigs that want a meal!

This activity enables children to:
✓ Learn about animal noises.
✓ Learn about pigs.
✓ Learn about rhyme.

What you do

Warm up
- Practise squeaking, squealing and oinking. Can you be very noisy pigs?

Activity
- Read the poem emphasizing the animal noise rhymes.
- Read through with the children. Be noisy hungry pigs!

Links

CLL LfC. 30-50m
- Join in with repeated refrains and anticipate key events and phrases in rhymes and stories.

CLL LfC. 40+m
- Listen with enjoyment and respond to stories, songs, music rhymes and poems and make up their own stories, songs rhymes and poems. (ELG)
- Extend their vocabulary, exploring the meanings and sounds of words.

CD CM&D. 30-50m
- Sing a few familiar songs.
- Explore and learn how sounds can be changed.

Talk about...
★ Animal noises. How many different animal noises can you make?
★ What do pigs look like? What colour are they?
★ What do pigs eat?
★ What do you like to eat when you are hungry?

Vocabulary
squeak   squeal   meal

Shout it out!

Oh the piggy-wiggy!

You put your right hoof in.
You put your right hoof out.
You put your right hoof in and you shake it all about.
You do the piggy-wiggy, And you turn around.
That's what it's all about!
Oink!

Oh the piggy-wiggy!
Oh the piggy-wiggy!
Oh the piggy-wiggy!
Oink! Oink! Oink!

You put your curly tail in.
You put your curly tail out.
You put your curly tail in and you shake it all about.
You do the piggy-wiggy, And you turn around.
That's what it's all about!
Oink!

This activity enables children to:

✓ Learn about parts of an animal's body.

✓ Become familiar with the concept of left and right.

✓ Use actions with a poem.

✓ Practise making the long 'o' sound.

Talk about...

★ Right and left. Which hand do you prefer to hold a crayon in?

★ What a pig looks like. Describe a pig's snout and his curly tail.

★ Where do pigs live? (in a sty)

What you do

Warm up

- Practise raising your left and right hand and putting out your left and right foot.
- Practise making a clear long 'o' sound by saying 'oh' 'oh' 'oh.'

Activity

- Read the poem demonstrating the actions and over emphasizing the long 'o' (oh).
- In a large space form a circle and sing the rhyme and do the actions.
- Shout 'oh!' nice and loudly.

Links

CLL LfC. 30-50m
- Join in with repeated refrains and anticipate key events and phrases in rhymes and stories.

CLL LfC. 40+m
- Listen with enjoyment and respond to stories, songs, music rhymes and poems and make up their own stories, songs rhymes and poems. (ELG)
- Extend their vocabulary, exploring the meanings and sounds of words.

CD CM&D. 30-50m
- Sing a few familiar songs.
- Explore and learn how sounds can be changed.

Vocabulary

right   left   hoof   curly   tail   sty   stable   barn

The cows in the field

The cows in the field go moo, moo, moo.
Moo, moo, moo, moo, moo, moo.
The cows in the field go moo, moo, moo,
All day long.

The pigs in the pen go oink, oink, oink.

The hens in the yard go cluck, cluck, cluck.

The ducks on the pond go quack, quack, quack.

The lambs in the meadow go baa, baa, baa.

The rabbits in the hutch go twitch, twitch, twitch.
(wiggle nose with finger)

This activity enables children to:

✓ Learn about animal noises.

✓ Produce animal sounds.

✓ Learn about a variety of animals.

What you do

Warm up

● Practise making animal noises: moo, oink, cluck, quack and baa.

Activity

● Sing the rhyme to the tune of 'the wheels on the bus'.

● Repeat with the children.

moo!

Talk about...

★ Other animal sounds. What noise does a cat, dog or mouse make?

★ Can you think of any other animal noises?

★ The names of the places where animals live e.g. pen, yard, hutch.

★ Other names for animal homes.

Links

CLL LfC. 30-50m

· Join in with repeated refrains and anticipate key events and phrases in rhymes and stories.

CLL LfC. 40+m

· Listen with enjoyment and respond to stories, songs, music rhymes and poems and make up their own stories, songs rhymes and poems. (ELG)

· Extend their vocabulary, exploring the meanings and sounds of words.

CD CM&D. 30-50m

· Sing a few familiar songs.

· Explore and learn how sounds can be changed.

Vocabulary

pond   yard   hutch   meadow   field

Tongue tricks

Reciting tongue twisters is an excellent way of learning to pronounce letter sounds and combinations clearly. It is enormous fun for children and practitioners alike. The fact that adults find tongue twisters just as tricky as children is often a source of amusement and creates a positive environment for learning literacy skills.

In this section you will find a variety of farm-themed tongue twisters. Each is accompanied by warm up exercises for the mouth that are both silly and fun but very important to tongue twisting success!

- ✓ The exercises focus on what we do with our teeth, tongue and lips to produce a sound or a series of sounds.

- ✓ The formation of each letter sound is summed up by a sentence that can be used as a mnemonic device (a way of remembering).

- ✓ The exercises lead up to a short tongue twister challenge, which, while achievable for adult and child alike, is still tricky enough to trip you up and induce a serious fit of the giggles!

Tongue twisters are difficult. The activities in this chapter are not designed to be achieved perfectly but rather are created for language fun. Playing with tongue twisters involves the acknowledgement of failure and the often hilarious struggle to master something that is very difficult. By striving to pronounce clearly alongside an adult, who is participating in the game as an equal, children can grow in confidence (and competitiveness!).

Remember

Children learn to produce speech sounds at different rates. Be positive and encouraging as attempts to articulate initial letters and blends are made. You are not making mistakes: you are having fun!

Pocket kitten

The 'k' and 'p' sounds

The 'k' sound is made by lifting the back of the tongue to the roof of the mouth. Air builds up behind the tongue and makes an exploding sound as the mouth is opened. The 'k' sound makes your breath kick!

The 'p' sound is made by pressing the lips together. Air is built up behind them and then as the mouth opens an exploding sound is made. The 'p' makes your breath pop!

Practise making 'k's and 'p's

- Hold your hand up in front of your mouth as you make the 'k' sound. Can you feel your breath on your hand as you make a quick, sharp 'k' kick sound?
- Make five 'k' kicks with your breath on your hand.
- Hold your hand in front of your mouth as you make the 'p' sound.
- Can you feel your breath as you make a quick sharp popping 'p' sound?
- Make five quick sharp 'p' pops with your breath on your hand.

Say: cup, cup, cup

Say: could you cuddle a cat?
      could you cuddle a cloud?

Say: pick, pick, pick

Say: piglets pick pears.
      piglets pick potatoes.

peeking
peeping

Links

CD CM&D. 30-50m.
- Explore and learn how sounds can be changed.

CLL LfC. 40+m
- Enjoy listening to and using spoken and written language, and readily use it in their play and learning. (ELG)

CLL LS&L. 30-50m
- Show awareness of rhyme and alliteration.

CLL LS&L. 40+m
- Hear and say the initial sound in words and know which letters represent some of the sounds.
- Hear and say sounds in words in the order in which they occur. (ELG)

Now your mouth has warmed up with all those 'p's and 'k's you are ready for the tongue twister.

Pocket kitten

The kitten in my pocket keeps peeking.

The kitten in my pocket keeps peeping.

Peeping, peeking, pocket kitten.

Please stop!

Bobby puppy

The 'p' and 'b' sounds

The 'p' sound is made by pressing the lips together. Air is built up behind them and then as the mouth opens an exploding sound is made.

The 'p' sound makes your breath pop!

The 'b' sound is made by pressing the lips together and then gently letting your breath bubble through them.

The 'b' sound blows beautiful bubbles!

Practise making 'p's and 'b's

- Hold your hand in front of your mouth as you make the 'p' sound. Can you feel your breath as you make a quick sharp popping 'p' sound?

- Make four quick sharp 'p' pops with your breath on your hand.

- Hold your hand in front of your mouth as you make the 'b' sound. Can you feel your breath as you make beautiful 'b' sounds?

- Make four bubble 'bs' on your hand

Say: pick, pick, pick

Say: pick up puppets

Say: bob, bob, bob

Say: bob, big, bubbles.

bubbles

Links

CD CM&D. 30-50m.

- Explore and learn how sounds can be changed.

CLL LfC. 40+m

- Enjoy listening to and using spoken and written language, and readily use it in their play. (ELG)

CLL LS&L. 30-50m

- Show awareness of rhyme and alliteration.

CLL LS&L. 40+m

- Hear and say the initial sound in words and know which letters represent some of the sounds.

- Hear and say sounds in words in the order in which they occur. (ELG)

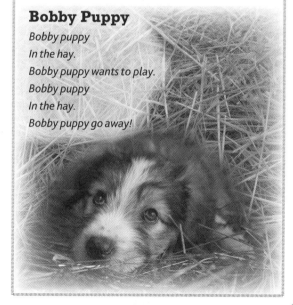

Now your mouth has warmed up with all those 'p's and 'b's you are ready for the tongue twister.

Bobby Puppy

Bobby puppy
In the hay.
Bobby puppy wants to play.
Bobby puppy
In the hay.
Bobby puppy go away!

Moo now, new cow

The 'm' and 'n' sounds

The 'm' sound is made by pressing your lips together and humming.
The 'm' sound hums.
mmmm mmmm mmmm

The 'n' sound is made by opening the mouth slightly, placing the tip of the tongue towards the front of the roof of the mouth and then bringing it down sharply.
The 'n' sound is nice not nasty!

Practise making 'm's and 'n's

- Press your lips together tightly and make a long 'mmmm' sound.
- Open your lips sharply after a count of three.
- Make four quick 'n' sounds.

Links

CD CM&D. 30-50m.

- Explore and learn how sounds can be changed.

CLL LfC. 40+m

- Enjoy listening to and using spoken and written language, and readily use it in their play. (ELG)

CLL LS&L. 30-50m

- Show awareness of rhyme and alliteration.

CLL LS&L. 40+m

- Hear and say the initial sound in words and know which letters represent some of the sounds.
- Hear and say sounds in words in the order in which they occur. (ELG)

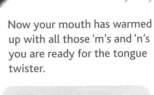

Say: mum, mum, mum

Say: mum makes muffins

Say: no, no, no

Say: no new nets.

Now your mouth has warmed up with all those 'm's and 'n's you are ready for the tongue twister.

Moo now

Moo now, new cow
Moo now, moo
Moo now, new cow
Moo new moos.

Silly sheep

The 's' and 'sh' sounds

The 's' sound is made by putting the teeth together and hissing air out between them.
The 's' sound makes you hiss!
Hiss, hiss, hiss, hiss

The 'sh' sound is made by opening your mouth and pushing the lips forward slightly, the teeth are then pushed together and air pushed through.
The 'sh' sound pushes and whooshes.

Practise making 's's and 'sh's

- Open your mouth, put your teeth together and hiss like a snake.
- Make four long hissing 's' sounds.
- Place you hand in front of your mouth and make four long hard 'sh' sounds.

ssshhhhh!

Links

CD CM&D. 30-50m.
- Explore and learn how sounds can be changed.

CLL LfC. 40+m
- Enjoy listening to and using spoken and written language, and readily use it in their play. (ELG)

CLL LS&L. 30-50m
- Show awareness of rhyme and alliteration.

CLL LS&L. 40+m
- Hear and say the initial sound in words and know which letters represent some of the sounds.
- Hear and say sounds in words in the order in which they occur. (ELG)

Say: sun, sun, sun

Say: sun, sea, sand

Say: shell, shell, shell

Say: shells shiver

Now your mouth has warmed up with all those 's's and 'sh's you are ready for the tongue twister.

Silly sheep

Silly sheep. Shhh!

Sally is asleep. Shhh!

Silly sheep. Shhh!

Don't you make a peep. Shhh!

Funny vet

The 'f' and 'v' sounds

The 'f' sound is made by placing your top teeth lightly in the middle of your lower lip and blowing.

The 'f' sound feels funny!

The 'v' sound is made by placing your top teeth firmly in the middle of your lower lip.

The 'v' sound is very vain.

Practise making 'f's and 'v's

- Can you make four funny 'f' sounds?
- Can you make four vain 'v' sounds?

Links

CD CM&D. 30-50m.

- Explore and learn how sounds can be changed.

CLL LfC. 40+m

- Enjoy listening to and using spoken and written language, and readily use it in their play. (ELG)

CLL LS&L. 30-50m

- Show awareness of rhyme and alliteration.

CLL LS&L. 40+m

- Hear and say the initial sound in words and know which letters represent some of the sounds.
- Hear and say sounds in words in the order in which they occur. (ELG)

Say: f

Say: fee fi fo fum

Say: v

Say: violet violin

very funny vet!

Now your mouth has warmed up with all those 'f's and 'v's you are ready for the tongue twister.

Very funny

Very funny is our farm.

Very funny is our vet.

Farm, vet.

Farm, vet.

How very funny can you get?

Don't touch!

The 'd' and 't' sounds

The 'd' sound is made by quickly touching the tip of the tongue to the roof of the mouth, just behind the teeth, and then dipping it back.

The 'd' sound dips and dives.

Place your hand lightly under your chin and make four dipping 'd' sounds

The 't' sound is made by putting your teeth together and then opening them.

The 't' sound makes your teeth tingle.

Place your hand in front of your mouth and make four 't' sounds. Feel your breath on your hand.

Say: do, do, do

Say: do, don't, do, don't

Say: tap, tap, tap

Say: tip, tap, tip, tap

Now your mouth has warmed up with all those 'ds' and 'ts' you are ready for the tongue twister.

Practise making 'd's and 't's

- Can you make four dipping 'd' sounds?
- Can you make four tingling 't' sounds?

can you say...

Don't touch
Don't touch the tractor
Don't touch the tractor
Don't touch the tractor
DON'T!

Links

CD CM&D. 30-50m.

- Explore and learn how sounds can be changed.

CLL LfC. 40+m

- Enjoy listening to and using spoken and written language, and readily use it in their play. (ELG)

CLL LS&L. 30-50m

- Show awareness of rhyme and alliteration.

CLL LS&L. 40+m

- Hear and say the initial sound in words and know which letters represent some of the sounds.
- Hear and say sounds in words in the order in which they occur. (ELG)

Run to the well

The 'r' and 'w' sounds

The 'r' sound is made by resting your top teeth just inside your bottom lip and then ripping them apart quickly.

The 'r' sound rests then rips!

Can you make four ripping 'r' sounds?

The 'w' sound is made forming the lips into a tight circle, then opening them.

The 'w' sound wishes you well.

Make four wishing 'w' sounds.

Practise making 'r's and 'w's

- Can you make four ripping r sounds?
- Can you make four wishing w sounds?

Now your mouth has warmed up with all those 'r's and 'w's you are ready for the tongue twister.

Say: run, run, run

Say: run, rabbit, run

Say: well, well, well

Say: wellies win, wellies win

Links

CD CM&D. 30-50m.
- Explore and learn how sounds can be changed.

CLL LfC. 40+m
- Enjoy listening to and using spoken and written language, and readily use it in their play. (ELG)

CLL LS&L. 30-50m
- Show awareness of rhyme and alliteration.

CLL LS&L. 40+m
- Hear and say the initial sound in words and know which letters represent some of the sounds.
- Hear and say sounds in words in the order in which they occur. (ELG)

Run, Run...

Run, run to the wishing well.

Wish a wish and wish it well.

Run, run to the wishing well.

Wish a wish and wish it well.

Let's tell stories!

The activities in this section encourage children to join in with the telling of a story. By allowing children to offer their own ideas and take the story in new directions the practitioner and the child engage in creative language play together. The practitioner offers a framework to support the child's ideas and encourages creative language development by reinforcing, extending, modelling and naming vocabulary.

Listening to stories helps children to:

✓ extend their vocabulary.

✓ experience a variety of linguistic constructions.

✓ enjoy creative language.

✓ have fun!

Telling stories helps children to:

✓ organize their thoughts.

✓ extend their vocabulary.

✓ learn to capture and hold the interest of the listener.

✓ sequence events.

✓ have fun!

Dialogic reading

What is dialogic reading?

Everyone loves stories. We love to listen to stories and we love to tell stories. Dialogic reading is where listening and telling are combined. It describes a learning situation where adult and child, or child and child, have a conversation about the story. Dialogic reading is based initially around three points.

1. Asking 'what' and 'where' questions

For example:

Adult: "What do you think the farmer is going to do next?"

Child: "He's going to feed the cows."

Adult: "Where do you think the cows are?"

Child: "The cows are in the field."

2. Asking open-ended questions

Avoid 'yes' 'no' answers. Open-ended questions often start with 'why'. Open-ended questions don't prompt a particular answer but are invitations to express an opinion or to encourage further discussion.

For example:

Adult: "Why do you think the calf is sad?"

Child: "He's sad because the sun has gone behind a cloud."

Adult: "Really? Why does that make him sad?"

Child: "I think he likes playing in the sun and now he feels cold."

3. Repeat and expand

A child's response is always valuable. Make sure they know this by repeating what they have said in whole or in part and using this opportunity to model correct grammar and pronunciation.

The introduction of new vocabulary is particularly effective in a dialogic reading situation. A new word can be introduced in context, in a focused situation and often with a picture to illustrate the word. Try to keep expanded phrases short to encourage repetition.

For example:

Child: "I tink dat dog is cared"

Adult: "Oh, really? You think that the dog is scared? Why do you think he is scared? Is he scared of the enormous cat?"

With very young children, the adult can take on both roles in the dialogue, modelling both question and answers.

Dialogic reading and picture books

Picture books provide a perfect opportunity for exploring a story together. Use picture books to encourage your children to:

- explore character's emotions. How does the character feel? What makes you think that?
- describe a situation in their own words.
- predict what is going to happen.

Dialogic reading without pictures

Picture books are a large part of story sharing in the early years. However, it is also important to tell stories without pictures.

By telling stories with words alone you are:

- allowing children to create their own images of the story.
- encouraging attentive listening.
- modelling oral story telling to the children.

Remember: Dialogic reading is shared reading, and sharing is above all about warmth and enjoyment. The most important thing you can do is to share your love of stories.

Some suggestions for stories suitable for dialogic reading

Farmer Duck
by Martin Waddell (Walker Books)

In the Country
by Benedict Blathwayt (OUP)

Little Red Hen
by Michael Forman (Red Fox)

The Snow Lamb
by Debi Gliori (Scholastic Hippo)

One farm
by Benedict Blathwayt (Red Fox)

Noisy farm
by Rod Campbell (Puffin)

Farmyard Hullabaloo!
by Gilles Andreae (Orchard)

Cluck a moodle farm series
by Julie Sykes (Hodder Children's Books)

Being a story teller

When telling a story:

- ✓ practise telling the story beforehand.
- ✓ be expressive – use your face and body to make the story come alive.
- ✓ use different voices to differentiate between characters.
- ✓ be dramatic – use pauses to heighten tension.
- ✓ look around the group as you tell the story. Use eye-sweeps to include every child.
- ✓ make eye contact with those who are finding it difficult to settle or whose attention may be wandering.

When reading from a book:

- ✓ if the story is new to you, look at it beforehand.
- ✓ decide on character voices beforehand (and be consistent!).
- ✓ if you there are no pictures to share, lay the book on your lap. Raise your head and speak to the group, dipping your eyes to read the next lines.

Sharing picture books with a group

There are certain practical difficulties in sharing a picture book with a group of children. Unless you are using a big book with a support frame it can be physically awkward to keep turning the book between yourself and the children. All too often, children at the periphery of the group spend too much time twisting, turning and fidgeting in order to see what is going on. If a child cannot see clearly they may become disengaged with the story.

Remember to:

- • familiarize yourself with the book beforehand. Make sure you know what is happening in each picture.
- • have a clear idea in your mind of the kinds of questions you are going to ask and the areas you are going to explore, but also be ready to take the talk in unexpected directions.
- • turn the book slowly at every stage so all children have a clear view.
- • check children's faces to ensure all are engaged with the book.
- • pay attention to those who may be losing focus. Try asking an open question to re-engage wandering minds.

On the Farm story templates

These farm themed story templates allow practitioners to create guided storytelling play. By offering a story structure practitioners can help children to:

- think logically and place events in sequence.
- imagine consequences to actions.
- model and expand vocabulary.
- feel a sense of ownership over a story.

Guided storytelling means that practitioner and child work together to create a story. It is important that you are flexible, allowing the children to make imaginative contributions no matter how unlikely the scenario becomes! However, it is important to remember your role as an educator as well as a facilitator.

Remember to:

- repeat a word or phrase, modeling the correct pronunciation.
- repeat a word or phrase that is an example of good language use.
- give praise to a reluctant or nervous contributor.
- follow up a child's suggestion with a further 'what' question.

'What' prompts

Use 'what' prompts to encourage creative thinking and extend vocabulary:

What colour was it?

What did it look like?

What did she do next?

What was he wearing?

What you do

- ✓ Gather your group of children and seat them.
- ✓ Tell the story, pausing and asking for suggestions where indicated.
- ✓ If the children are reluctant to contribute, draw suggestions on a whiteboard or on paper. Don't worry, your drawings don't have to be accurate; they are prompts that help stimulate discussion. If you tried to draw a castle and a child shouts out "it's an elephant", say: "that's brilliant; you think they arrived at an elephant. What colour is it do you think?"

Remember to:

- show respect and enthusiasm for all suggestions.
- repeat each child's suggestion clearly, extending and developing vocabulary and grammar if necessary. Repeat once, while looking directly at the child and then again to the whole group.
- speak clearly, varying your tone and pitch to make the story exciting and engaging.

Story template 1:
Farmyard adventure

Once upon a time there were four animals friends: Cat, Dog, Horse and Duck. They lived together happily on a little farm. One day they decided to set off on an adventure to see what the world was like.

They each packed a bag for the journey.

What do you think they took?

They set off into the farmyard.

Who do you think they met?

They then saw three paths. One path led to the hills. One path led to the river. One path led to a barn.

Where did they choose to go?

What did they find there?

They became hungry and sat down to eat their food.

What did they have to eat?

As the sun set over the countryside the friends went back to their lovely little home. They were very tired after such a busy day, so they stretched and they yawned and they fell fast sleep.

Having a lovely time!

Links *for all story templates*

CLL LfC. 30-50m
- Listen to stories with increasing attention and recall.
- Describe main story settings, vents and principal characters.

CLL Reading. 30-50m
- Begin to be aware of the ways stories are structured.
- Suggest how a story might end.

Story template 2:
The runaway tractor

Once upon a time, in a rickety shed in the corner of the farmyard, there was an old tractor.

What colour do you think it was?

The old tractor was bored. She wanted an adventure, so she started her engine and trundled out of the shed.

The farmyard had three gates, leading to three roads. One led to the fields. One lead to the forest and one led to the town.

Which road did she take?

After a while she met someone walking along the side of the road.

Who do you think it was?

Suddenly it started to rain and big puddles appeared on the road. It was raining so hard that the tractor couldn't see where she was going. There was a bang and a pop.

What had the tractor bumped into?

What did she do next?

Finally it stopped raining. The little tractor decided that it was getting late and that she better continue her adventure another day so she turned around and headed back to her little tractor shed.

Story template 3:
What will Munton do next?

Munton the mole lives in a hole in the middle of the three-corner field.

Moles have very, very tiny eyes and they have very, very big paws. Moles can't see well but they are very good at hearing sounds, and they are extremely good at feeling things with their big front paws. Today Munton has decided to go for a walk. He puts out his paws, feels his way to his front door, opens it, and goes out into the field.

What is the first thing he feels with his feet?

Munton listens very carefully. He can hear an animal making a noise.

What kind of animal is it?

What noise is it making?

Munton is getting hungry now. He digs his big paws into the ground and pulls out a long wriggly worm. He slurps it up. Yum!

What is the worm like?

He walks a little further and comes to the edge of the field.

What does he find?

Where does he go next?

Munton is getting tired. He starts to yawn. He walks back across the field, finds his front door and is very pleased to be back home again.

Story sequencing

The ability to organise a story into a beginning, a middle and an end can be difficult for young children. You may find that children remember the most exciting part of a story or focus on a particular aspect that appeals to them. By practising story sequencing skills children learn to:

- organise their thoughts clearly.
- attend to narrative.
- improve their ability to comprehend.
- understand the concept of consequences.
- recollect facts and incidents.
- articulate their thoughts clearly.
- manage practical tasks.

The following suggestions are for practical farm-themed sequencing activities and include making story cards, picture books and story sacks.

Sequencing cards

Make sequencing cards for your favourite farm stories.
You don't have to be good at drawing – be resourceful!
Find relevant pictures in magazines or on the internet.

What you need

- ✓ A farm themed story
- ✓ Thick card
- ✓ Pens /pencils/ found images
- ✓ Glue
- ✓ Scissors

What you do

- Choose a story with a simple plot. Break the narrative into sections and decide on the images that go with each point in the plot.
- If you have broken down your story into six main points, cut out six squares of card (approx 8cm x 8cm).
- Draw/paste images of each of the plot points on the cards.
- Laminate the cards if you can.
- Tell the story to the children.

The life cycle of a frog

It's not only fictional stories that can be sequenced. Animal life cycles, instructional activities and natural events are all excellent material for creating sequencing activities. Talk about the life of a tadpole and make tadpole sequencing cards or represent the cycle in dough or clay.

Sample text for sequencing activity

- Frogs lay eggs. This is called frogspawn. Frogspawn is a collection of clear jelly like eggs. In the middle of each clear egg is a little black dot. That dot is going to be a tadpole.
- Each dot grows into a tadpole. At first a tadpole has just a body and tail.
- It then grows legs, while it looses its tail.
- The legs get larger and the body changes colour and shape.
- Finally the tadpole changes into a frog. It can now spend time on land as well as in water.

Tadpole sequencing cards

What you do

- Cut five squares of card (8cm x 8cm).
- Draw each stage of a frog's development on each card.
- Laminate each card if possible.
- Talk about the life cycle of the frog with the children.
- Show picture of frogspawn, if available. Look on the Internet or in library books for examples.
- Ask the children to sequence the cards.
- Discuss their choices. Do you all agree?

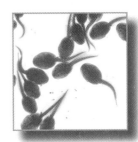

Dough tadpoles that turn into frogs

What you **do**

- Talk about the life cycle of a frog.
- Look at pictures of frogspawn, tadpoles and frogs.
- Ask children to model the life cycle of a frog using clay.
- Start with a small lump of clay for the egg then add more clay to gradually give it legs.
- Increase the size and create a frog

Links *for all frog activities*

CLL LfT. 40+m

- Begin to make patterns in their experience through linking cause and effect, sequencing, ordering and grouping.
- Begin to use talk instead of action to rehearse, reorder and reflect on past experience, linking significant events from own experience and from stories, paying attention to how events lead into one another.

CLL Reading. 40+m

- Retell narratives in the correct sequence drawing on language patterns of stories. (ELG)

KUW Time. 30-50m

- Talk about past and future events.
- Develop an understanding of growth and decay and changes over time.

Make your own farm picture book

Make your own book about farms and farming. Display it where everyone can see it. Give it to each child in turn to take it home to show parents and carers, and make it easily available for language play in and around your setting.

Making your own book enables children to:
- Understand how books are created.
- Talk about what they have seen.
- Make decisions and organise their thoughts.
- Put events into sequence.
- Place objects in categories.

What you do

- A book about your own visit to a farm.
- A book about different types of animals on the farm.
- A book about farm machinery or farm buildings.

What you need

✓ A4 card
✓ Toy farm animals
✓ Hole punch
✓ Treasury tags
✓ Farm pictures

Talk about...

Initiate a discussion about what kind of book or books you could make. Remember, when leading discussions with the very young, it's important to respond to and appreciate all contributions. Repeat suggestions to the whole group, modeling correct grammar and pronunciation.

Links

CLL Reading. 30-50m
- Know information can be relayed in the form of print.
- Show interest in illustrations and print in books and print in the environment.

CLL Reading. 40+m
- Know that information can be retrieved from books and computers.

Make your own farm story sacks

Story sacks are very popular in early years settings. They are available commercially but are fun to put together yourself. Story sacks usually contain a book and items and characters relevant to the story. In this activity, however, the book is missing. Instead, children take out a series of farm-themed objects in turn and create a story around them.

What you do

- Seat the children.
- Say, "Once upon a time there was a…"
- Choose a child to take two items out of the sack.
- Ask for story suggestions about the two items.
- Continue taking one or two items out at a time asking the question, "What happened next?"
- Suggest story ideas yourself until children become confident with their own suggestions.
- When the last items have been withdrawn ask for endings to the story.

What you need

- ✓ A sack or draw string bag
- ✓ Farm-themed items (at least 10). These can be toys or items from small world play or even pictures.

Links

CLL LfT. 30-50m

- Use talk to connect ideas explain what is happening and anticipate what might happen next.

CLL LfC. 30-50m

- Describe main story settings, events and principal characters.
- Use a widening range of words to express or elaborate on ideas.

Let's pretend!

Children learn and develop language in a social context. This means that language learning is active learning – children 'do' talk. Pretend play or role-play allows children to 'do' talk while exploring a situation they are in control of and feel comfortable with.

Role-play

Role-play is an important way for young children to develop and practise language skills. By participating in role-play children:

- ✓ Learn subject specific vocabulary.

- ✓ Learn the importance of talk in a given situation.

- ✓ Use observational and recall skills to remember and reproduce a situation or series of actions.

- ✓ Understand the feelings and needs of others.

- ✓ Listen to others and follow up on what has been said.

Practitioners can offer farm scenarios, prompts and props to encourage farm-themed role-play fun. It's useful if you can visit a farm to see what happens firsthand, but if that isn't possible, learn about roles and activities from books, magazines or DVDs.

Remember...

Don't worry too much about having the right role-play equipment. Children often explore complex and creative role-playing scenarios with no physical prompts or props at all. Sometimes all that is needed to inspire role-play is exposure to the initial role itself.

Section 5

Farm visits

Visiting a farm is a memorable occasion for a young child. There is so much to see and so much to talk about. Many open farms offer visits that are well structured and that are accompanied by age appropriate activities. Practitioners can benefit from this and add to the experience by developing their own follow up activities.

Keeping it in mind
(ways to remember your visit)

- Take photographs.
- Collect souvenirs.
- Take sketchbooks.

Retelling

It's important to retell the experience as soon as possible after the visit. Use your photographs, souvenirs and sketches to recall the visit.

Talk about...

- What the children did. Can they retell the day in sequence?
- Favourite animals.
- What they liked/didn't like doing.
- What the weather was like.
- What the farm smelled like.

Idea maps

Idea maps are a useful way of exploring a topic orally while making a connection with literacy. Using a whiteboard during your discussion, write down key vocabulary, repeating it orally as you write it. This will reinforce vocabulary and show that writing can represent thought.

Watching DVDs

If a farm visit isn't possible for you, watch a DVD or read a story with pictures about life on a farm. Retelling activities can be carried out in the same way. (See also *What if we had a farm?* Featherstone).

Let's pretend!

Farm shop role-play

Many farms have shops where they sell their produce. They may sell:

- Eggs from their chickens
- Meat from their cows, sheep, chickens and pigs
- Sausages in lots of flavours
- Burgers
- Pies and pasties
- Homemade cakes
- Homemade jam
- Honey from bees

What you need

- ✓ A venue for the shop (a table top is good)
- ✓ Money
- ✓ A till
- ✓ Produce (see below)

What you do

Make produce for your farm shop with:

- dough.
- empty boxes.
- empty plastic jars.
- real hard boiled eggs.

Links *for all role-play activities*

CD DI&IP. 30-50m

- Engage in imaginative play and role-play based on own firsthand experience.
- Notice what adults do, imitating what is observed and then doing it spontaneously when the adult is not there.

KUW Place. 30-50m.

- Show an interest in the world in which they live.

Talk about...

- ★ Farm shops. Who might be in a farm shop? What might they be doing?
- ★ What is your favourite type of food? Would it be sold in a farm shop?
- ★ Do you like jam? What flavour do you like best?

Feeding time role-play

Feeding time is one of the busiest times on the farm. All the animals need their breakfast... so do the farm workers!

What you need

- ✓ Toy animals (or children can role-play animals themselves)
- ✓ Shredded newspaper for hay
- ✓ Bowls and bags for carrying food
- ✓ Baby bottles
- ✓ Ride-on vehicles for tractors

Talk about...

- ★ Feeding animals.
- ★ Calves and lambs may need bottle feeding.
- ★ Cows and horses need fresh hay.
- ★ Chickens and ducks need grain.
- ★ A tractor may need to carry hay up to the fields.
- ★ Farm workers may need bacon and eggs in the kitchen.

Making hay

Hay is messy! Pretend hay is messy, but it is very useful when role-playing farms. It can be fed to animals, used as bedding and shaped to form a nest for chickens and ducks. Use shredded newspaper or scrap paper to make hay. Keep a dustpan and brush handy!

Let's pretend!

Role-play farm vet

Vets have a very important role to play on the farm. When animals become sick they make them better, and they are there to lend a hand when baby animals are born.

What you need

- ✓ A large vet's bag
- ✓ Empty plastic bottle for medicine
- ✓ A spoon
- ✓ A thermometer
- ✓ Blankets to keep poorly animals warm
- ✓ Toy animals (or children can role-play animals themselves)

Talk about...

- ★ The role of a vet on the farm.
- ★ What might they carry in their bag?
- ★ What might be wrong with some of the animals? A broken leg or wing? A cold or cough?

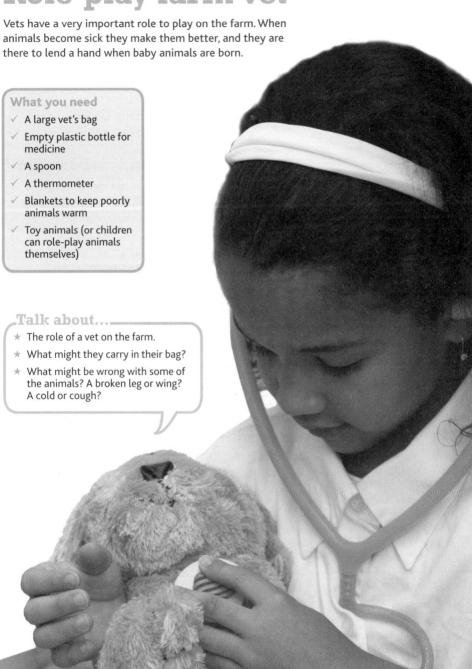

Let's perform!

Producing a performance is fun. It allows children to develop confidence as individuals, encourages them to work together in a group and to feel a sense of belonging to the class as a whole. A successful performance brings an unbeatable sense of triumph. Performance is an excellent way for young children to learn to speak clearly and with confidence. Children who can articulate clearly have enhanced phonic awareness, reinforcing reading, writing and spelling skills. A performance most of all is a great opportunity to present new knowledge and skills in an entertaining and informative way.

Learning a line of a rhyme is something children do well. It's done spontaneously and naturally in play when children sing nursery rhymes or playground chants. Children may find it more difficult to say their line or lines at the correct time. Coming in at the right time is an important skill to practise. It teaches children to listen carefully to what has been said before and see their speech as part of a whole.

In the following play one or two lines can be given to each child. Use your professional judgement to decide who should be given a certain line or lines.

Let's pretend!

Morning on the farm

(A play in rhyming couplets)

(All make animal noises count to 5 and then stop.)

Wakey, wakey, rise and shine.
On the farm it's feeding time!

The farmer has what she likes most:
A cup of tea and some buttered toast.
(slurp tea, munch toast)

The cockerel is very hungry too.
He shouts 'cock-a-doodle-doo!'

The chickens need food to lay their eggs.
They peck at the corn and they stretch their legs.
(act like chickens)

The cows are by the barn where they're milked each day.
They're ready for some water and some nice fresh hay.
(moooooo)

The horses in the stable are waiting for their oats.
It gives them glossy manes and lovely shiny coats.
(neigh, stamp feet)

Up the hill is a field of sheep.
So we're off in the tractor – beep, beep, beep!

The ducks on the pond like to eat snails.
They flap their wings and they wiggle their tails.
(quack, quack, quack)

The pigs in the pen squeak and squeal.
They make this noise for every meal.
(oink, oink, oink)

Tess the sheep dog runs in the yard.
She needs her food because she works very hard.
(woof, woof, woof)

All the animals munch, munch, munch.
But very soon they'll be asking if it's…
Time for lunch!

(All make animal noises to count of four then 'cock-a-doodle-doo' in unison)

Language games

for chatty children and lovely listeners

Many early years games promote speaking and listening skills. Speaking
and listening is at the heart of learning in the early years and the early
years practitioner takes every opportunity to focus on developing those
skills in his or her children, whatever the activity. In this section you will
find farm-themed games that promote specific speaking and listening
skills from sound discrimination to turn-taking skills.

Sound discrimination

The ability to discriminate between sounds is vital
to clear speech production and comprehension.
Children are exposed to all sorts of sounds:
environmental sounds, speech sounds, musical
sounds and animal sounds.

Environmental sounds

The world is full of sounds. Sometimes it's difficult
to discriminate between different environmental
sounds. Look around your setting and listen for
the sounds that emerge when no one is talking.

You may hear:

- ✓ Chair legs scraping on the floor.
- ✓ Water running from the tap.
- ✓ The whirring of a computer.
- ✓ Sand being poured into a tray.
- ✓ Wheels of ride-on toys going round.
- ✓ Bricks being snapped and stacked.
- ✓ Crayons being dropped into a container.
- ✓ A felt pen writing on a whiteboard.

Munton the mole

To encourage children to speak clearly and listen carefully, make Munton the mole and incorporate him into activities in your setting.

Unfortunately Munton cannot see very well. But he does have a great sense of hearing

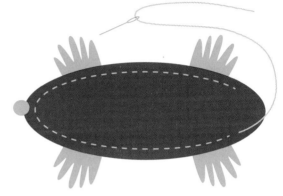

What you need
- ✓ Black velvet or fur fabric
- ✓ Old tights for stuffing
- ✓ Needle and thread
- ✓ Pink felt

What you do

- Cut two large ovals of the same size out of the fabric and place wrong side to wrong side.

- Stitch all the way round, leaving a gap of about four centimeters.

- Turn inside out so the velvety/furry side is now on the outside.

- Stuff with old tights and sew up the gap.

- Cut a small circle of pink felt for the nose and stitch in place.

- If you are feeling particularly creative cut four 'hand' shapes from the pink felt and stitch in place.

- Encourage them to explain their activities to Munton and to check if he is listening carefully.

Links

CLL LfC. 30-50m
- Listen to others in one-to-one or small groups when conversation interests them.

CLL LfC. 40+m
- Speak clearly and audibly with confidence and control and show awareness of the listener. (ELG)

Section 6

'Rabbity ears' game

The rabbits on the farm are quiet creatures. They like peace and quiet. Unfortunately their big floppy ears can hear every sound around them.

What you need

✓ Elastic
✓ Cardboard
✓ Scissors

What you do

- Make floppy rabbit ears.
- Cut out two long rabbit ear shapes from card.
- Thread elastic through the base of each.
- Make sure the elastic is long enough to tie securely but comfortably under a child's chin.
- Make enough pairs of rabbit ears for each child.
- Seat the children quietly.
- All put on rabbit ears, close eyes and twitch noses like rabbits.
- One person carries out an activity that makes some noise.
- Ask for hands up and guesses as to what the person did.

You could:

- Walk across the floor heavily then turn on a tap.
- Turn on the computer.
- Open a packet of crisps and crunch them up.
- Find a crayon in a crayon box and draw a picture.

Links

PSED D&A. 40+m

- Maintain attention, concentrate and sit quietly when appropriate. (ELG)

Further fun

Put on your rabbit ears and stand or sit quietly outside.

What can you hear?

'Tick tock where's the clock?' game

Tick tock, where's the clock?
It's time to doodle-doo
Tick tock, where's the clock?
Who'll doodle, me or you?

What you need

✓ A variety of small clocks or stop watches that tick (analogue not digital)

What you do

- Place the clocks around your setting. It is best if you place them behind other objects rather than in drawers so that the ticking sound can be heard.

- Practise being cockerels. Scratch around the floor and when you raise your hand the children shout 'cock-a-doodle-doo!'

- Recite the 'tick tock' rhyme.

- Then very quietly tip toe around seeing if you can find the clock.

- When a clock is found shout 'cock-a-doodle-doo!'

cock-a-doodle-doo!

Links

PSED D&A. 40+m

- Maintain attention, concentrate and sit quietly when appropriate. (ELG)

Farm percussion

Clapping hands, stamping feet and slapping knees are all ways of producing non-vocal sounds. Percussion instruments are also readily available to the early years practitioner from educational suppliers. Drums, shakers, rattles and chimes can be made through junk play.

This activity encourages children to listen carefully to the sounds that you are making and reproduce them themselves. The practitioner tells a story that is illustrated by percussion sound patterns. The children repeat each of these sound patterns with their instruments and bodies.

What you need

✓ Shakers – one per child and one for you. (Empty small water bottles half filled with dried peas are ideal, but any shaker will do.)
✓ Your bodies!

What you do

● Seat the children.
● Hand out one shaker each.
● Explain to the children that you'd like to see if they can copy exactly what you do.
● Read the story, 'On the farm'.

On the farm

Farmer Kate put on her boots and stamped across the farmyard.

(Stamp four times. Children copy with four stamps.)

She picked up a bucket of corn.

(Shake shaker three times. Children copy.)

She opened the door to the chicken shed and saw…

A fox frightening her chickens!

She clapped her hands loudly.

(Clap three times. Children copy.)

The fox ran out.

(Drum feet quickly on the floor to the count of five.)

She called to the chickens to come out.

(Slap hands on knees four times.)

Farmer Kate threw the corn on the ground for the chickens.

(Shake shaker rapidly.)

Suddenly the fox jumped back in and the hens all flew up to the roof, the fox ran around in the corn and Farmer Kate clapped her hands. What a noise!

(Shake shakers, stamp feet and clap hands.)

Links

CD CM&D. 30–50m
· Explore and learn how sounds can be changed.

CD CM&D. 40+m
· Explore the different sounds of instruments.

Sound-scape orchestra

Create an amazing recording of farm sounds as you become a sound-scape orchestra.

What you do

- Discuss with the children the different types of noise you might hear on a farm such as:

★ gates creaking	★ tractor engines brumming
★ boots stamping	★ ducks quacking
★ cows mooing	★ chickens clucking
★ sheep bleating	★ buckets clattering
★ cocks crowing	★ dogs barking
★ horses neighing	★ pigs snorting

What you need

- ✓ A whiteboard or paper for recording ideas
- ✓ A baton or stick for the conductor (you!)

- Brainstorm your farm sounds and write them up on a board or large sheet of paper.
- Assign pairs or small groups of children a particular sound.
- Decide how that sound could be produced. Animal noises can be produced vocally. Other mechanical sounds such as a gate creaking could be made by rubbing metal together.
- Experiment until you are happy with your sounds.
- Seat the sound-makers in clusters according to their noise.
- Tell the children that they can only make their noise while you are pointing at them with your baton (stick).
- Conduct your orchestra!

Links

CD CM&D. 30-50m

- Explore and learn how sounds can be changed.

CD CM&D. 40+m

- Explore the different sounds of instruments.

Record your orchestra and play back your sound-scape as a backdrop to farm play.

Hide and sheep

This game enables children to practise both receiving and giving instructions. Practising instructional talk through play helps children to think logically and to put events in order.

What you do

- Choose one child to be the sheep dog.
- Blindfold the sheep dog.
- Hide the sheep somewhere in your setting, making sure that the rest of the children see you doing this.
- Take the blindfold off the sheepdog.
- Explain to the children that they must not tell the sheepdog where the sheep is.
- They then must tell the sheep dog to go forwards, backwards, up, down, or side to side until he or she finds the hidden sheep.

What you need

✓ A toy sheep. (You could also use a beanbag or pompom.)

Links

PSRN SS&M. 30-50m
- Observe and use positional language.

PSRN SS&M. 40+m.
- Find items from positional or directional clues.

Animal sounds poem

What you need
✓ A group of children
✓ Your voices

What you do
- Recite this poem with plenty of noisy animal sounds and guess the animal at the end of each verse, then play some animal sounds games.

Who's there?

We've all come to the farm to play.
Who's in the barn today?

I say moo, I don't know how
I give tasty milk.
I am a... cow!

Quack, quack, you are in luck.
I swim on the pond.
I am a... duck!

Oink, oink I am quite big.
I'm often pink.
I am a... pig!

Neigh, neigh, you can ride on my back of course.
I eat oats and hay.
I am a... horse!

Meow, meow. Give me a pat.
I'm very furry.
I am a... cat!

Baa baa. My wool you can keep.
Baa baa.
I am a... sheep!

Cluck, cluck, I scratch in my pen.
I lay eggs.
I am a... hen!

Links

PSD D&A. 30-50m.
- Seek and delight in new experiences.

CLL LS&L. 30-50m
- Enjoy rhyming and rhythmic activities.

Farm animal sounds game

What you need

- ✓ A group of children
- ✓ Your voices

Links

CLL LS&L. 30-50m

- Enjoy rhyming and rhythmic activities.
- Show awareness of rhyme and alliteration.
- Recognise rhythm in spoken words.

What you do

- Seat the children in a circle.
- One child makes an animal noise (moo, oink etc) and then says the name of another child in the circle.
- That child then says the name of the animal that made the noise.
- The child then makes a noise of their own and names another child.
- If a child is feeling too shy to make a noise or can't guess the animal, move quickly on to another child.

mooo!

oink!

baaa!